New Gl

Written by Elspeth Graham
Illustrated by Mal Peet

Collins Educational
An imprint of HarperCollins*Publishers*

Would you like...

red glasses?

Blue glasses?

Green glasses?

Yellow glasses?

I'd like red and blue and
green and yellow glasses.

I like my new glasses.